Carols

to Jean Ashworth Bartle
and The Toronto
Children's Chorus

TWO CAROLS

1. Hey! Now   2. Farewell! Advent

Late 15th-century English poem

BOB CHILCOTT

'Hey! Now' and 'Farewell! Advent' are the first and third in a set of three carols commissioned in 1994 by Jean Ashworth Bartle and the Toronto Children's Chorus. The second is the upper-voice version of 'Mid-winter', available separately (T121) from Oxford University Press. The three carols may be performed separately or as a set. An orchestral version of the accompaniment for each of the three carols is available for hire from the publisher, scoring: 1. ('Hey! Now') 2.2.2.2.– 2.2.0.0.– cym. + glock.– hp.– str. 2. ('Mid-winter') 2.2.2.2.– 2.0.0.0.– 0.– hp.– str.; 3. ('Farewell! Advent') 2.2.2.2.– 2.2.0.0.– glock.– hp.– str.

Printed in Great Britain

OXFORD UNIVERSITY PRESS, MUSIC DEPARTMENT, WALTON STREET, OXFORD OX2 6DP

Sweet

Je-sus is come to us, this good time of Christ-mas._____

Where-fore with praise sing we al-ways, 'Wel-come, our Mes - si - ah!__

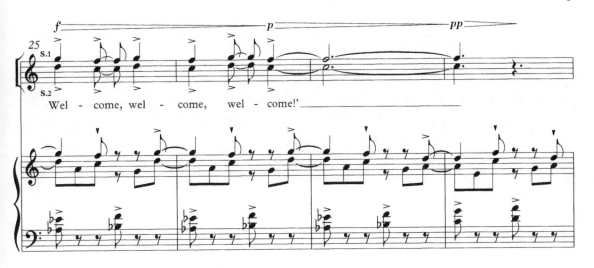

Wel - come, wel - come, wel - come!'

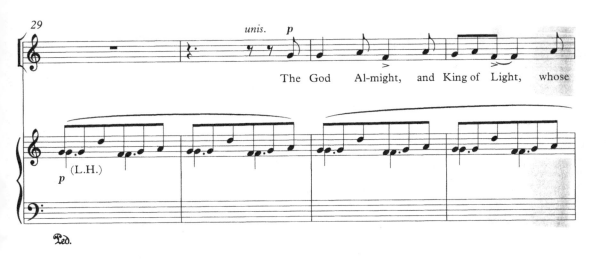

The God Al-might, and King of Light, whose

power is o - ver all,____ Give us, of grace, for

to pur-chase His realm ce-les - ti - al.

Where his an - gels and arch-an - gels do sing in-

-ces-sant-ly, His___ prin - ci-pates and po -tes-tates make great har - mo-

-ry, ke - ry.

The ver - tues clear their tu-nès bare, their choir for to re - pair; Whose

song to hold was man - i - fold of do - mi - na - tions fair. With

one ac - cord_ serve we that Lord with laudes and o - rai - son._ The

which hath sent, by good as - sent,_ to us his on - ly son._

2. Farewell! Advent

James Ryman (15th century)

BOB CHILCOTT

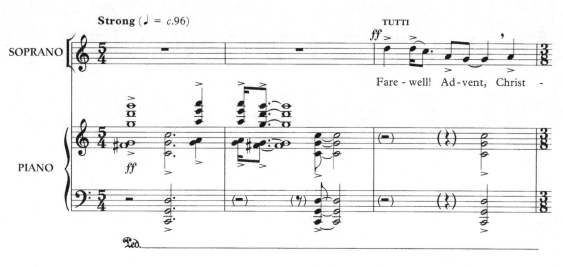

bone and skin; there - fore our love thou shalt not win—

Fare - well from us both all and some. Our

bread was brown, our ale was thin, our bread was mus - ty

* 'At the birth of the King of all.'

ISBN 0-19-342615

Music origination by Barnes Music Engraving Ltd., East Sussex
Printed in Great Britain by Halstan & Co. Ltd., Amersham, Bucks.

9 780193 426153